CORRUPTION IN CHINA

Meditations on Salary, Mistresses,
Confucianism, and Chinese Academia

by
Thorsten Pattberg

I0202400

**lod
press
new
york**

Printed in the United States

ISBN: 0-9842091-9-0
ISBN-13: 978-0-9842091-9-4

Four timeless and thought-provoking essays by German writer and cultural critic Thorsten Pattberg on Chinese corruption during the Xi Jinping era, addressing the problems of full salary, mistress culture, new Confucianism, and rampant cronyism in China's academia.

THORSTEN PATTBERG

CORRUPTION IN CHINA

BEIJING - Li Keqiang, the new premier of China, vowed to "tackle corruption" and "clear government," which includes — mind you — most schools, hospitals, banks, universities, companies, public transport, the courts and the police. In unison, Li also wants to "double the average income," and now is the time, I think, to elaborate on the fact that, technically, China has no concept of "full salary" (some call it living wage) in the sense it developed in the West alongside the idea of human rights.

Just like in Europe in the feudal days, the typical Chinese public servant today drags himself around with little or no money, and thus stays close to his master. In the past that was the emperor, now it is the party.

Corruption isn't just political, it's now personal: It is the people who feel exploited, disrespected, not valued, not paid enough, and who feel truly frustrated, hopeless and sorry for their families, so they go out and take what they can. The Chinese do not trust each other anymore.

Teachers, students, office clerks, officers, professors, even governors, no one gets more than 30 to 40 percent of the living wage they would need to pursue their actual duty full-time, letting alone caring for themselves, or raising a family. The rest, they have to "earn" by other means, often by hidden perks or through abusing their power; and if one thing can be said about the Chinese elites after the Cultural Revolution is that they are survivors. Let us first talk about the concept of 发票 *fapiao* (invoice/receipt).

In a typical Chinese environment where everyone lacks money but the mother lode is rich, the only way to get the money out of her register is by handing in a fapiao for exchange — an invoice for cash reimbursement. Experienced senior cadres will present fapiao for their business trips, stationary, electronics, watches, public transport, karaoke, dating, gifts and, most important, always lavish and excessive food for their business partners and friends.

That's why there are so many unnecessary conference centers, high-end hotels, KTVs (karaoke bars), and restaurants that are offensively costly (even for international standard) and outright unaffordable (if it were to be paid from one's own pocket). The same is true for the vehicle fleets and housing. A private 70-sq.- meter flat in Beijing costs at least 10,000 yuan per month. But the wage of a senior judge or professor is just 7,000 yuan per month before tax; so he often depends on free housing from the government. Needless to say, those flats are highly competitive, and only *guanxi* (connections) are known to speed up the process.

Most governmental institutions have built their own adjoined hotels, karaoke bars, massage parlors, and restaurants serving crab dinner, so that fapiao can be issued to the local bosses; a perfect symbiosis. They recently sacked an official in Zhejiang Province who brought in 832,200 yuan of fapiao; 20 times that of his actual "salary."

Foreigners who wish to invest in China should first learn about the salary situation of the

Chinese host, that the Chinese are paid poorly and that they must be corrupt for a living. Thus the Chinese official will have to cash into the foreign investment for his private expenses in order to survive, and this isn't a metaphor. Even if he cannot put his hands on the foreign investment, or receive gifts or bribery, he will explore all means of Chinese hospitality, conferences, shark fin lunch, and foot massages, thus will indulge the high-flyer life of the moment, all on his organization's or the government's bill. Naturally, the Chinese host will want to bring his friends into this, and lengthen the negotiations.

Foreign businessmen often assume that China is low-budget, only to pay through the nose — every time. That's because they compare average salaries in China — barely $500 a month. Had they studied the culture, however, they would have realized that those figures are not "full salary," and that the foreign visitor, indirectly through the hospitality, is another source of income.

Everyone who worked in China has (often embarrassing) experience with corrupt officials, who earn less than they deserve, and much less than they feel they deserve; and thus transform into sly entrepreneurs.

How else could they afford cars, homes, furniture, luxury goods, Harvard education for their kids (you have no idea), or traveling abroad? Asking for salary is considered bad sport, and it is still a tradition in Chinese elite universities, for example, that doctors and post doctors live without meaningful income well into their forties (and intermarry) — a modern version of the imperial eunuchs: They live on allowance for campus food and subsidized on-campus lodgings.

Some Chinese commentators, and most foreign companies that operate in China, will argue that, according to the law of supply, there are simply too many Chinese on the market, making their labor cheap. Often, you don't have to pay them wages at all; covering their minimum living existence is quite suffice; like the contracted migrant workers who sleep on bunk beds and shower only once a week.

To this I reply that we would still need to have some universal concept of "living wages," just like we need to have a "concept of human rights," because otherwise, simply put, China will never learn to respect human dignity, and may one day even decide that foreigners (the other 80 percent of the world) can be seen as "plenty and cheap" too. Already, we have Westerners lined up in China who are paid extremely low wages, yet who are often morally unprepared to triple or quadruple their income the way the Chinese do.

Foreigners should not work underpaid just "because the Chinese do," and foreign CEOs certainly shouldn't pay tribute and risk their good reputation for the dubious practice of being invited by some almighty party officials to a full-blown state dinner banquet, knowing that the official would not and could not pay for such acts of debauchery if it were to come out his own pockets.

Still others tell me that it has to do with Confucian values; that a humble wage was emblematic of the gentleman (*junzi*) who would find other ways to make the job "pay" anyway because the culture was inclined toward nepotism, entitlement, and taking advantage of officialdom.

Li wants to curb all of it: "reduce the number of people on the payroll; stop excessive official overseas travels," he said, and "no construction of government halls and buildings, less hospitality and fewer purchases of fleets of cars."

What is China going to do with all that excess savings on money? Here's an idea: Pay out a "full salary" so that the people will get an incentive at least to imagine a world without corruption.

DANGERS OF A
NEW CONFUCIANISM

BEIJING - There have been rumors in recent months about the possibility of a revival of *rujia* or Confucianism in China. Powerful scholars, not without their personal agendas, have called for a Confucian constitution.

A lot of people have likened Xi Jinping's concept of the *zhongguomeng* or Chinese dream, and his rejuvenation of the Chinese nation, to the teachings of the Great sage. There are even voices that claim that Mr. Xi's recent 'Anti-Corruption Campaign', including a massive clampdown on the sex trade in Dongguan, Guangdong province, can be directly attributed to the Confucian cause of constructing a *hexie shehui* or harmonious society led by *haoren* or uncorrupt men. [1]

Reading Confucius is, of course, fascinating; just like reading the works of Socrates, Plato, or any other archaic thinker. Their aphorisms are general, simple and most basic - how can their words not be true? It can even be argued, then, that certain elements of the Greco-Roman tradition always remained with Europe, such as the emphasis on individualism, freedom, and reason. Similarly, certain Confucian values such as filial piety, the love for learning, and a lofty pragmatism have prevailed in modern China. Some cultural traits, or shall we say cultural preferences, such as ancestor worship and self-cultivation are so deeply engrained in the Chinese tradition, that they go without saying Confucius.

However, I have a notion that actions such as the crackdown on prostitution and the curbing of rampant corruption are based on reason and a common sense of modern statesmanship. They should not be attributed to the recommendations of Jesus Christ, the Buddha, Confucius, or any other wiseman who lived in the first millennium BC.

Confucianism, a 2,500-year-old tradition, is anything but uncorrupt -from a modern perspective. It is about hierarchies, patriarchy, nepotism, abuse of officialdom, pure inequality and moral dictatorship. Many social critics, including Lu Xun, Mao Zedong, the vast majority of European philosophers and historians, not to mention scholars from Japan –a nation which has prominently distanced itself from the Chinese yoke- have argued that Confucianism was the main reason for China's cultural backwardness. In fact, China may be so corrupt today not despite the Confucian legacy but because of it.

The Confucian Canon, often referred to as a code of conduct rather than a proper religion, could essentially be seen as an instruction manual for cult leaders and dictators on how to morally blackmail the people into submission. Hence the absence of universal concepts of freedom, individualism, and human rights - although there's a lot of talk about human responsibilities such as piety, obedience, and conformity.

As a rule, in a Confucian society you don't want to be the butt of society, but belong to the privileged, aristocratic elite –the learned and superior 君子 *junzi*. The large majority of the people are kept in place as moral slaves absolutely dependent on the sages' wisespeak.

The vibrant sex trade and mistress culture that are now haunting modern China and blemishing its image in the world, instead of being the result of communist ideology or capitalist vice, might as well be the direct expression of the out-dated, yet undefeated Confucian way: the entitlement of superior men and their exploitative life style.

To be true, ever since its founding in 1921, the Communist Party of China fiercely opposed and battled the anachronisms of the Confucian heritage such as polygamy, concubinage, arranged marriages, and widespread mistress culture among China's elites.

It may take forever to establish the rule of law in China precisely because Confucius believed that coercing people with a sense of moral obligation, shame, and "face" works better than laws and punishments. He was wrong. His teachings elevated a few elites, and made them enslave the rest of the people, with the unenviable consequence that for thousands of years, in the words of German philosopher Georg Wilhelm Friedrich Hegel, the large majority of the Chinese cherished "the meanest opinion of themselves, and believe that they are born only to drag the car of Imperial Power."

More than a few China experts have suggested that the troubled Communist Party under Xi Jinping, instead of dashing into an unknown future of liberal democracy and Westernization with Chinese characteristics, may want to revive Confucianism in order to justify its authoritarian grip on power. As I said, Confucianism works perfect at that: The Confucian ideal of a government run by supreme human beings with supposedly superior moral values, not dissimilar to Plato's fascist philosopher kings, is possibly the greatest corruption of all.

Note:

1. China's Crackdown On Sex Trade: An Anti-Corruption Campaign in Disguise?, *Forbes*, Feb 21, 2014

ON CHINESE MISTRESS CULTURE

BEIJING - There is something I must tell you about China: It is rather morally creative in the usage of its women.

There isn't a hotel, massage parlor, ktv, or conference hall in town that isn't frequented by "little sisters" (xiaojie), escort personnel (baopo), hostesses (peinv), or other types of prostitutes (jinv). There's a name for any relationship a female plaything may fall into:

Here are the "second wives" (er laopo), women [who may have family or kids but] who indulge in extramarital affairs with men, married or not. Then we have "the thirds" (disanzhe) who are casual love affairs only.

The queen of all female roles, however - in direct competition with the faithful "wife" (laopo)- is the "mistress" (qingren). The mistress, a femme fatal, not only embodies adventure and carnal pleasures, but is also the surest status symbol a man can wish for: She shows you have money.

13

Technically, only married men can have mistresses; otherwise, if the gentleman is single, we would refer to his female company - however many of them- as simple "girlfriends" (nvpengyou). The Chinese tradition of maintaining mistresses is based on what good Christians would refer to as adultery - a sin; yet in China it is mere custom - a habit.

Consequently, when Westerners first come to China, they are utterly perplexed by the strict division here between marriage, romance, and sex - for which, in Chinese thinking, of course (at least) three different types of women are required.

Xu Qiya, a Jiangsu party official, had clearly set a local record with 140 mistresses; we know because he kept a sex diary. But he isn't an inventor: In fact, I have yet to meet a dulcet Chinese girl who has not been offered a gift from a married man at some time. At least, that's what they told me.

Accepting any gift from a married man, whether it being a handbag, a blue box from Tiffany & Co., a car, a trip to the beaches of

Hainan, is the unspoken agreement of becoming the mistress of that benefactor. It is the lure and excitement of an extraordinary lifestyle - luxurious, free, illicit, and irresponsible - that drives ever more 20-somethings not to marry, or at least to postpone marriage until their bodies become less marketable.

Those entrepreneurial women, of course, fill the pool of potential future mistresses in China to the brim. If a woman is not married by the age of 26, she "expired" and is usually stigmatized as "leftover woman" (shengnv).

Now let us talk about the situation of the Chinese married man. Post-marital infidelity is encouraged in China just as pre-marital sex is encouraged in Europe. In comparison to the West, only very few wives in China will file for divorce upon discovery of their husband's infidelity. It is rather sad.

In China, sex and power are a pair. State-run *Xinhua News* recently found that 95% of all corrupt officials in China also kept mistresses. And Tom Doctoroff, an economist, estimates that second wives probably account for one-third of China's entire consumption of luxury goods.

Let us talk about China's capital, Beijing. From top to bottom, it isn't a place for connubial happiness: It's a very patriarchal society (there is mistress culture, but no such things as mister culture), and some of the most powerful men, including the Communist Party of China, create and procreate here, trailed by legions of businessmen, scholars, diplomats, and entrepreneurs, who mostly see no problem in renting a maid for warming their pillows.

In fact, the magazine *Business Insider* quoted a vice-ministerial-level official who insisted that "there is no official at his level who doesn't have at least a few lovers." It is a must-have.

The victim is the young woman of China. As her feelings for any particular man dwindles (they are all cheaters, no?), she too becomes emotionally detached, and regards being a mistress as a form of business, or transactions of favors - a form of consumerism.

There are several grades of "maintaining" (baoyang) a mistress: The cheapest, of course, is to bed a university student. She is young, flexible, poor, and full of romantic ideas in her head. She will eventually marry a fellow classmate, but until then she may want to sneak out and bag a sugar daddy in Wudaokou, Zhongguancun, or Shaoyang district.

Next is the working woman. She is independent, has experience, and owns or rents her own place. She might even be married, but, with her husband banging the next hostess at the local karaoke bar, she probably thinks what the heck.

Perhaps the highest cost of maintenance goes to the trophy mistress (huaping, a "flower pot"). Her goal and profession is to conquer the most powerful man she can find at a time. It's a life-style - it's her religion. Enormous financial resources, and a good amount of drama, are necessary to snag such a high-profile gold digger.

It has been observed that many Chinese women opt out of the Chinese tradition of cheating husbands and try to find a foreigner, preferably from a traditional monogamous society like Western Europe. Those "foreigners" (laowai) may also cheat on their spouse, of course, but for individual reasons, not, as is the case in China, as a social prescription or norm.

And so the mistress culture of China lives on, from vulgar to lustrous and glittering, and if the endless supply of young women for successful men does not ebb - and if women don't divorce - the husband and his lovers will happily drive the market for luxury goods, hotel rooms, and publications about mistresses, and, almost as an afterthought, minister to their ethical ruin.

.

CHINA'S OBSESSION WITH HARVARD AND THE IVY LEAGUE

BEIJING - It is no secret that the Chinese have a crush on Harvard. Naturally, high intelligence is drawn to elite universities like physical strength to top sports. And with overwhelming evidence from the social sciences that East-Asians, on average, have a higher IQ-score than Whites (which results in higher SAT-scores throughout the United States, of course), ivory towers now have come to salute outstanding Chinese applicants on a scale unprecedented in history. Harvard has de facto become a Chinese outpost.

It is not alone. Whether it is the University of California, Berkeley, Yale University, or Cambridge University in the UK; those top schools brim with Chinese prodigies, relatives, princelings, or else engage in China-related research and cultural diplomacy. Good for China's elites, but there is a dark side to it: brain drain.

The latest piece of evidence comes from a $15 million donation to Harvard by a billionaire couple, Pan Shiyi and Zhang Xin, in order to establish a 'Soho China Scholarship'. This wasn't at all that newsworthy because Chinese donations like this to Harvard are somewhat common, but this one in particular sparked outrage on Chinese social media (or was it a well-orchestrated publicity campaign?).

As business people, apart from the Soho name's sake and patronage, Mr. Pan and Ms. Zhang surely expect some form of return on their investment, probably by getting one of their own into Harvard: a family member, a relative, a friend, many friends —who knows. Most Chinese commentators would have little problems with academic rent-seeking, as the caring for one's family and friends is an inherent component of the Chinese tradition. In fact, most critics would probably do the same if only they had the monetary means.

Xi Jinping, the country's president, sent his daughter to Harvard; and Bo Xilai, the former major of Chongqing, had his son enroll at

Harvard's John F. Kennedy School of Government, where he made headlines for his extravagant lifestyle: the cars, the ladies. This all confirmed what international observers had already suspected: That China's *taizidang*, the sons and daughters of China's rulers, are droning into the US Ivy League mainly for the *guanxi* and the prestige, rather than for the pursuit of deeper educational ideals or higher truths, letting alone academic careers. The critics' ultimate concern, however, is this: Why not investing into China's education?

Chinese students, together with other East-Asians such as Singaporeans, Japanese, and South Koreans, have on average superior mathematics, reading, and science skills. This is readily available facts. No one is in the dark any longer. Even the UN study of the OECD's 'Programme for International Student Assessment' (PISA) confirms that much: students from Shanghai, Macao, Hong Kong, and Taipei are on top of the world. Why not their universities?

There is something particularly alluring to China in this American passion for Ivy League, world rankings, and elite education. That Americans indulgence in this extreme segregation of their society into the privileged 1% and 99% human soup is painful to watch, but a deep-seated problem in all Anglo-Saxon cultures. After all, the Anglo-British still have their monarchs, the unelected House of Lords, upper-class grammar schools such as Eton, Charterhouse, and Harrow, and the snobbish world of Oxbridge.

In such a pathological class society, education isn't about knowledge, if it ever was, but about privilege. The books on the shelves are all the same. What is studied doesn't matter as much as where it is studied. US and British elite universities have thus turned into an exclusive club frequented by the US/UK ruling classes, academic dynasties, the global plutocracy, Chinese top officials, the Jewish connection, Eastern princes and Arab sheiks, and the sons and daughters of India's Brahmin cast.

That said, since there are so many well-to-do Chinese students (China has more dollar millionaires than Germany, Britain, and Japan combined) they scatter and trickle down to second and third tier US universities: in 2013, over 235,500 of them, according to the Institute for International Education. In the educational American hinterland they quickly get bored, they party, they buy expensive cars, or help relatives with local businesses. Compared to their high-flying compatriots in the US Ivy League, they clearly got the lesser deal; but, still, whatever the Chinese do, even if it's doing nothing extraordinary, combined with all those American-born Chinese already in the country, they are greatly increasing the average IQ in their respective US district or county. It's a big win for the United States.

This has alarmed parents and guardians of other minority crowds in the country, and prompted a famous American scholar at Yale Law School, Cai Mei'er, later joined by her Jewish husband, to write best-sellers about allegedly superior cultural attitudes. That scholar goes by the name Amy Chua, alias "the

Tiger Mom." Her writings are quite intimidating: Professor Chua, a former graduate of Harvard College, asserts that Chinese mothers are *superior* and more successful in the United States (her daughter, need I say this, also attends Harvard) due to a strange cocktail of superiority complex, insecurity, and impulse control –the so-called 'triple package'. That's of course putting the cart before the horse: The Chinese in China are not a stressed-out minority group trying to overcompensate against a dominant white majority, yet their children, too, have high IQ scores.

Cambridge University in England is another case in point. The dons just love the Chinese. Cambridge recently made headlines again because of a whopping £3.7 million donation by no other than Wen Ruchun, the daughter of former Chinese Prime Minister Wen Jiabao. The donation was non-transparent, made through a shadowy 'Chong Hua Foundation' based in off-shore Bermuda. Ms Wen made international headlines the year before in a bribery probe to Morgan Stanley, the US Investment Bank. The bankers bribed Ms. Wen, and would always bribe her, time and again, because that's apparently the thing-to-do when doing business in China –in case you lived the last thirty years of red capitalism in a cave.

Apart from a brief public outcry, the deans of Cambridge had no objections to Chinese money that's now being used for a good cause, namely for funding a prestigious chair, allowing generous travel grants to friends and colleagues, and maintaining a culture of wining, dining, and doing favors. And, who can blame them? Oxbridge depends on its China connection just as Morgan Stanley does, and brims with ego at the prospect of invaluable sinecures and perks which are, after all, the butter and bread of academic existence.

England is a tiny country, and its economy is dwarfed by China, Japan, Germany, and even France. Yet its institutions of higher education are world-class. In order to make sure that this remains so, Cambridge University and other top schools such as Oxford, LSE, or SOAS are cunningly planning for the future of their prestigious candy shops: No less than the sons and daughters of the world's elites are being groomed and pampered here. Unsurprisingly, they are willing to pay any price for the treat.

Not to appear tight and ungrateful, Great Britain sometimes does offer financial support, upon proof that the candidate doesn't really need it, which goes into the pockets of spoiled Chinese students who are by definition already from China's upper social strata. And because China is not a Western-style democracy but a party dictatorship, the Chinese elites are far more affluent than their European peers. They rarely need financial aid at all, but are naturally grateful for another title gracing their superhuman cvs; to the dismal of Japanese students, by the way, who get little to none financial support based on the fact that Japan is labeled a 'developed' country whereas China is not. In fact, as if it were the world government, Oxbridge is heavily selecting its overseas students by merits of their nationality and geopolitical calculation that further segregates the overall student body.

At most major British universities there are now international dormitories packed with Chinese students and those who look like them - literally East-Asian ghettos.

This UK's desperation for rich and powerful Chinese customers didn't get unnoticed in China's megacities, where university freshmen already joke about which British school to pick from for their graduate studies —Oxford or Cambridge? Neither of those institutions is considered particularly difficult; in fact, they are considered a sham; a British sale scheme really: You book a One-Year-Master Program that everyone who pays passes. (In China a Master takes two or three years). Consequently, few applicants make even the slightest attempt to conceal their motives that they are solely interested in the convenience and brand.

Moreover, English universities are far less competitive and selective than, say, Peking University, Tsinghua University, or Fudan University of China, all of which require Chinese candidates to score well into the top

0.1% of the *Gaokao* national entrance examination in any given year.

Naturally, Chinese see a degree from Britain as some kind of real-time English course with a museum attached to it. And yes, they are also planning on visiting Europe's Berlin, Madrid, Paris, and Venice during their free time, of which there will be plenty. To which the cynic could reply, of course, that all those British surplus MAs, MScs, and PhDs were artificially created and dumped-down just for a very particular well-to-do East-Asian clientele. Education is big business.

The Chinese understand that very well. In fact, there are hundreds of 'agencies' in Beijing, in Haidian district alone, that help students prepare their application packages, including a fine resume, brilliant essays, and even flattering recommendation letters for going abroad. Most of those services are very successful, even hiring Western expats and professors as senior editors. UK admission officers have no way to verify a single thing on those application forms, which in all probability: almost none of it was entirely written by the candidate alone. Not that they cared anyway since Chinese who can afford such expensive services and put an enormous effort into their perfect, fabricated application are most likely the same Chinese who will succeed in university and in life at large.

Beijing, meanwhile, is pushing hard to reverse the brain drain. Tsinghua University, for instance, has attracted a $300 million donation from the US-based Schwarzman Group as part of an initiative to train "future world leaders." Tsinghua boasts some of the finest engineering and sciences departments in the country, and is often dubbed "the MIT of China." It is wealthier than Peking University –known as PKU or Beida– or Renmin University, its two main Beijing competitors. Tsinghua prides itself with having produced Xi Jinping, China's current president and autocratic leader, as well as hundreds of other technocrats that entered the Communist Party and now run China.

Peking University isn't holding back either. In 2010, it hired the former Director of Harvard

Yenching Institute, Tu Weiming. The American-Chinese 'Confucian Ethicist' acts as if he was the pope of China. He became a legend for having paved the way into Harvard for hundreds of Chinese elites. Now those elites are big in China, and have built an almost cult-like network of adulation, loyalty, and mutual support.

Few outsiders understand the political game of elite academia, be that in America, Britain, or China: the necessary nepotism, the cronyism, and the patriarchy that keep it all together. Prestigious and charismatic leaders rake in millions of dollars, from government and businesses, that they must spend on generous conferences, favorable publications, and idiosyncratic projects, comparable to lobbying for congress or running a syndicate. And if they don't do it, someone else will come and drag all those resources away.

There is an unspoken agreement that Peking University will invite any Harvard Professor who is willing to visit Beijing for a guest lecture; and is expecting them to return the favor. In fact, it is hard to find anyone at Peking University in a top position who has not yet been to Harvard at some point during his career. Hence the byname "Harvard of China."

In its eternal competition with Tsinghua, Beida now announced the establishment of its own "future world leaders" program -the Yenching Academy. Top PKU leaders headed by Party Secretary Zhu Shanlu, a good friend of Harvard, and university president Wang Enge, who was a visiting professor at Harvard, mandated that the center of the University, Jing-yuan Courtyard, is going to be renovated to house and groom 100 chosen graduate students –the so-called future "Yenching Scholars," expressing a strong desire of the Peking committee to be linguistically affiliated with the Harvard Yenching Scholars at Harvard University.

Those prestige projects are but the drums of a new dynasty: China's so-called C9 League wants to go toe-to-toe with the American Ivy League –by parasiting it. Already, Harvard in Cambridge, Boston, of Massachusetts, looks rather small and provincial compared to the mega universities in Beijing, China's political, cultural, and financial capital with a population greater than that of the Netherlands or Australia. Peking University, China's mother lode of higher education, has three, four, and five-star hotels that charge up to $500 a night, dozens of restaurants, moonlight and stardust conference centers, and even built an entire 'New Global Village' with 3,600 rental units for foreign visitors. And while Harvard may be filthy rich, better equipped, and more international, largely thanks to 200 years of US imperialism, the United States are but a sub-culture of the European tradition, while Beijing represents the nucleus of an ancient civilization: It simply is the greater phenomenon.

China needs, no wait, it deserves its own Harvard (and Cambridge, Yale, Princeton…). It is entirely conceivable precisely because Chinese students have momentum and a competitive advantage, which currently spurns them into succeeding anywhere in the world. But as long as the elites in China don't believe in their own civilization and would rather invest their wealth in education elsewhere, nothing short of a miracle is needed to wake a billion people and this once so proud nation from their deeply historical slumber.

ABOUT THE AUTHOR

Thorsten Pattberg (裴德思 Pei Desi) is a German writer, linguist, and cultural critic.

He has written and published extensively about Global language, Competition for terminologies, and the End of translation. He is also active in promoting Confucianism, in particular Chinese terminologies, on a global scale.

Dr. Pattberg attended Edinburgh University, Fudan University, Tokyo University, and Harvard University, and earned his doctorate degree from The Institute of World Literature at Peking University. He studied under the guiding stars of Ji Xianlin, Gu Zhengkun, and Tu Weiming, whom he considers his spiritual masters.

Currently a Visiting Fellow at the Institute for Advanced Studies on Asia, University of Tokyo; Dr. Pattberg is a former Research Fellow at the Institute for Advanced Humanistic Studies, Peking University. He is the author of four monographs 'The East-West dichotomy,' 'Shengren,' 'Holy Confucius,' and

'Inside Peking University,' and some of his representative articles are 'Language hegemony – It's shengren, stupid!,' 'Long into the West's dragon business,' 'China: Lost in Translation,' and 'The end of translation.'

Dr. Pattberg's writings have appeared in *Asia Times*, *China Daily*, *Global Times*, *Global Research*, *Corbett Report*, *China Today*, *Shanghai Daily*, *Die Zeit* (German Times), *Korea Herald*, *The Korea Times*, *Taipei Times*, *South China Morning Post*, *Southern Weekly*, *People's Daily*, *The Diplomat*, *Dissident Voice*, *Thought Catalog*, *Big Think*, *RT Russia*, and *The Japan Time*. He has given public lectures in five countries and is a member of several academic associations such as the International Association of Comparative Mythology (IACM), the German East Asiatic Society (OAG), and the International Association for Comparative Study of China and The West (IACSCW).

He is a native of North Rhine-Westphalia, the City of Hamm.

www.ingramcontent.com/pod-product-compliance
Lightning Source LLC
Chambersburg PA
CBHW071940020426
42331CB00010B/2945